Stone Roses

Stone Roses

Poems by

~~Linda Neal Reising~~

Linda Neal Reising

Cover design by Shay Culligan
Cover art by Dave Malan

ISBN: 978-1-954353-14-5

Kelsay Books
502 South 1040 East, A-119
American Fork, Utah, 84003

To Irma Neal, my mother,
Jeanne Neal Jackson, my sister,
Hope Staubitz, my daughter,
and Reid Neal Staubitz, my heart—
all descendants of "stone roses"

To Mark Williams, Jessica Thompson,
Teresa Roy, Tom Raithel, and Barbara Bennett—
my friends who encouraged me throughout this project

Foreword

This collection of poems first started taking shape in my mind when I read the book entitled *Women Who Pioneered Oklahoma: Stories from the WPA Narratives* (University of Oklahoma Press), edited by Terri M. Baker and Connie Henshaw. Within this collection of narratives, I could feel the strength and determination of the women who made Oklahoma, my home state, into the place it is today. I could also hear the echoes of my own family stories.

My father's family was driven to Oklahoma from Tennessee on the Trail of Tears, so I could understand the pain of the women who told of their own families' forced removal. My maternal grandmother lived in a sod house when she was a child, so I could empathize with the women who lived in deplorable conditions, battling snakes and insects. And my second great-grandmother, living on her Cherokee allotment in Delaware County, witnessed the death of her young husband when he was attacked by bandits on his way home from purchasing grain for their livestock. His horses brought him home with a dagger driven through his neck, but not before he shot one of the attackers. It was fascinating to read, in these accounts, that others shared the same history of confronting lawlessness and loss. Over and over, as I read the interviews and worked on these poems, I could hear the voices of my own ancestors.

Of course, the WPA stories stand on their own, as they were originally recorded by the interviewers. However, I wanted to give the women more voice than was revealed in the short excerpts. I also gave the women names—fictional ones—since they were kept anonymous when their narratives were written down. In doing so, I tried to select names that were appropriate for the time period. I also chose to keep the labels and birth dates of the women as they were recorded because those descriptions add context to the stories they tell.

It is my hope that these poems, like the original interviews, will remind people of the sacrifices that the pioneers, specifically women pioneers, made in creating the state of Oklahoma and in settling the country as a whole. It is also my hope that I have inherited at least some small fragment of the grit and courage seen in these "stone roses."

Contents

Naomi (Miami—b. 1877)   13
Emmaline (Anglo—b. 1867)   14
Daisy (Cherokee Freedwoman—b. 1852)   15
Ida Mae (Anglo—No birth date)   16
Lena (Sac & Fox—No birth date)   17
Grace (Anglo—b. 1877)   18
Clementine (Anglo—b. 1861)   19
Talulah (Choctaw—No birth date)   20
Maude (Anglo—b. 1855)   21
Minnie (Cherokee—b. 1851)   22
Henrietta (Cherokee Freedwoman—b. 1852)   23
Sally (Anglo—b. 1869)   24
Hattie (Cherokee—b. 1840)   25
Violet (Anglo—b. 1868)   26
Ola (Chickasaw—b. No birth date)   27
Nettie (Cherokee—b. 1851)   28
Edna (Anglo—No birth date)   29
Alberta (Anglo—b. 1862)   30
Inola (Cherokee—b. 1887)   31
Florence (Anglo—b. 1881)   32
Cora (Choctaw Freedwoman—b. 1857)   33
Augusta (Anglo—b. 1857)   34
Jennie (Choctaw/Chickasaw—b. 1883)   35
Rose (Anglo—b. 1870)   37
Nannie (Cherokee—b. 1877)   39
Lizzie (Anglo—b. 1867)   40
Winema (Modoc—b. 1872)   41
Vera (Anglo—b. 1872)   42
Josie (Cherokee—b. 1887)   43
Iva (Anglo—b. 1855)   44
Lottie (Choctaw Freedwoman—b. 1859)   45
Sadie (Anglo—b. 1889)   47

Inez (Choctaw—b. No birth date)   48
Pearl (Anglo—b. 1870)   49
Birdie (Cherokee—b. 1877)   51
Sarah (Anglo—b. 1874)   52
Mary (Euchee—b. Between 1846-1851)   53
Dora (Anglo—b. 1855)   55
Mahala (Cherokee—b. 1877)   56
Maggie (Anglo—b. 1868)   57
Nell (Delaware—b. No birth date)   58
Helen (Anglo—b. 1855)   59
Ruby (Chickasaw—b. 1837)   60
Ruth (Anglo—b. No birth date)   61
Beulah (Cherokee/Chickasaw—b. 1837)   63
Tillie (Cherokee—b. 1887)   64
Esther (Anglo—b. 1883)   65
Awinita (Cherokee—b. 1878)   66

Naomi (Miami—b. 1877)

I am one of the last—the last of the full-bloods.
Born in Indiana, land of the Indians, I was moved
to the town in Oklahoma that shares my Nation's
name. As a girl, I was sent to Chilocco,
near the Kansas border, where Indians
from every tribe had white ways drummed
into them. First, they cut the boys' hair—black
snakes sunning on the floor—then scrubbed
us all with kerosene, liquid fire that burned
and sickened us with its smell. They forced
the girls into stays that stilled breath to shallow
gasps, the boys marshalled into military
uniforms. Worst of all, they took our tongues,
lashed us with bugle blasts, forced us to stand
at attention for hours if we were caught
using our old language. Yes, we were trained
to be farmers and housewives, bakers
and seamstresses, but mostly we were trained
to forget.

Emmaline (Anglo—b. 1867)

The prairie thrummed with hooves, bellows
filling the dung-thick air, pumped
from the lungs of frenzied cattle
surrounding the wagon, herds
turning old Wagoner Pasture
into an ocean of muscle and horn,
a tide of coarse hide undulating
as far as the eye could see. My son,
barely two, cried, clung to my shirt,
while I, with callused hands—
leather holding leather—pressed
the reins against my palms, pressed
on to the West, fearing lightning
strike or bobcat scream that might
drive beasts to madness, leaving
two more unmarked mounds, waiting
to be covered by sage grass, green
waves cresting knee-high and singing
a song as sad as an ancient sea dirge.

Daisy (Cherokee Freedwoman—b. 1852)

My folks belonged to Deward Randolph,
so I was born a slave at a place called Caney,
just southeast of Tahlequah. We raised
wheat and Hungarian millet,
gathered blades off corn and bound them
in bundles for fodder. Our masters
were kind—strong horses to ride,
good whiskey to drink, and plenty meat
to eat. But I envied the slave children
at the Landrum place, where Mistress
taught them to read and write, do sums
in their heads. When I was ten,
Mr. Deward put me in the back
of a buckboard, drove me to the home
of Colonel William Penn Adair, famous
Cherokee lawyer. After a handshake,
he left me there, and I trembled
in the August heat, knowing my mother
was lost to me. Years later, freed,
I learned Mr. Deward had been sued,
and Colonel presented his defense.
Me? I was nothing but chattel,
worth no more than a barrister's fee.

Ida Mae (Anglo—No birth date)

Women looking to marry
came to Muskogee by train—
black beast belching soot, smoke—
and were greeted at the station
by swarms of townsfolk, including
one reporter from the only newspaper
in town, a mousy man, licking
his pencil, taking down names—
those just plowing through,
those sinking roots into this red clay.

Even the girls who in Tennessee
would never be considered belles
could find a young lawyer to court
or some other ambitious beau
enticed to this new land, Indian
Territory, one moccasin
in wilderness, one shoe
in polite society. Any girl with grit
and letter of introduction
could wed in a wink.

The night I arrived, a storm
threw a chivaree—rattling branches,
shaking rooftops. The morning
after, there were no streets,
only rivers, but I did not mind
because rivers meant plenty
of fish, waiting to be caught.

Lena (Sac & Fox—No birth date)

It is hard to fight an enemy the eye cannot see.
It is impossible to know, when one welcomes
a stranger, that his name is Death. A Kickapoo
came to the Territory from Mexico, and my people
invited him to stay. He brought gifts—blankets,
silver trinkets, a case of black small pox.
The children suffered the most, their precious
skin marred by raging rash, and their mouths
too sore to swallow milk. It was common for five
or more people to die in a day. The grave
diggers could not work fast enough, so they dug
large holes, dumped the bodies in, letting them
land as they might before covering them up.
All along the banks of Euchee Creek, the mounds
of mass burial grew. And still, to this day,
they rise up in remembrance, sometimes
offering up a baby tooth, a tiny finger bone.

Grace (Anglo—b. 1877)

All of my family, the whole clan that was left
after the Civil War, came up to this country.
Grandmother had never learned to do anything
in her life but look pretty, bathing in milk
and rubbing her skin with rose water and glycerin.
But after the war, when the family was left poor
and all the slaves were freed, she felt the need
to be useful, no longer an ornament decorating
a grand plantation house. She became a midwife,
riding a hundred miles or more over the rocks
and through the creeks to bring a child into this life.
For twenty years, she boiled rags, scalded
knives, bathed faces of scared young women
who knew the cemetery was full of their kind.
And all this time, Grandmother never lost one,
neither mother nor child. Never charged a cent
for saving the lives of many because they
had saved her, too, changing her from a Southern
belle, fussing over a smudge on her white lace
glove, to a warrior woman, clipping the cord
of a newborn, challenging Death to a duel.

Clementine (Anglo—b. 1861)

We walked across the meadow
of prairie paintbrush to a gathering
of our Indian neighbors, assembled
for a *cry*. First, we feasted on pashofa—
pearl hominy and stewed pork—
served in bowls with horn spoons.
Then a preacher, convert from the old
ways, moved away from the long board
table, mounted a tree stump, and began
to thump his Bible, reminding us all
how we once lived in darkness
of sin but now we knew the light
of Christ. His dark eyes smoldered
with the fervor of an ancient
prophet. Then he led us to a spot
near a cedar tree, its limbs trimmed
with blue beads. In its shadow
stood a cross over a grave, the grass
just beginning to cover the rocky
scrabble a year after burial.
Women, their black hair falling
around their faces like mourning
curtains, moved forward. One
opened her mouth, let loose
a high, sorrowful sound,
and the others took up the cry,
singing so sadly that even the dead,
listening under the ground,
must have felt a tear slipping
from beneath closed lids.

Talulah (Choctaw—No birth date)

Cholera claimed the Honey King,
father of my grandfather, on the Trail
to the Territory. Little Blue Hen,
his wife, stayed with him 'til the end,
watching the wagons cross the Ouachita,
leaving her with three boys, the youngest
a baby swaddled in her paisley shawl.
The older two, ten and twelve,
cut long stem grass for a bed,
gathered wood and pine knots,
built a circle of fire to fend off
wolves and panthers who voiced
the screams Little Blue Hen swallowed.
When his soul passed, the three
used sticks and knives to dig a grave,
piled dead limbs and rocks on top,
blazed the trees all around to mark
the site. Then they fed on roots,
wild berries, corn flour, before sipping
honey from a spoon, communion
in honor of his sweet memory.

Maude (Anglo—b. 1855)

We lived in a mansion as far as dugouts go—
two windows of wavy glass, two rooms,
rock fireplace on one end. Money—we did not need
much except for flour, sugar, coffee. Sometimes
calico or shoes for the children. Most was grown
on our land. My husband would hunt quail—
two hundred at a time—and sell them in Vernon,
a dollar a dozen, along with my eggs for five cents
and butter fifteen cents a pound. In '97,
we planted cotton, sold nine bales at four cents
a pound. Yes, we were rich until we were not.

Then we hitched the team to the wagon,
went out on the prairie where dried bones
of buffalo shone white in the sunlight.
All day we worked, hoisting remains
of ribs and thighs, heaping the wagon,
a half ton of skeletons, three dollars' worth,
waiting to be ground, to feed the soil
of some distant farmer who never heard
the bellow, felt the quake of stampede.
Or to be turned into fine bone china,
a teacup raised to the lips of a wealthy
woman in New York who would never
know she kissed the bones of bison.

Minnie (Cherokee—b. 1851)

My uncle, a white man from Texas,
was the blackest soul I ever met. Hard to believe
he shared my father's blood, two men
as different as cast iron and cotton. My uncle,
a man of means, was mean to his core
when it came to caring for his slaves.
He worked them from sunup to long past
moonrise, riding his Palomino among the crop
rows, using his crop to strike out at any weary
worker stopping to stretch. Coiled around the horn
of his horse's saddle—a whip of tanned leather,
a black snake waiting to strike. One day,
while I played beneath a mulberry tree, I heard
Uncle cursing a young slave named Clem,
who had dipped from the water bucket
before the bell to stop had rung. He told the slave
to take off his shirt, wrap his arms around
a fence post. His whip cracked the air, cracked
open Clem's back with stripes of red, the young
man's screams silencing the birds. Suddenly,
I heard a loud war whoop, and an Indian
appeared like a spirit, lunging his Paint at Uncle,
then drawing his quirt across the cursed
man's eye, blinding him more than he already was.
The brave lowered his hand to Clem, pulled him
up behind, and rode away. When I ran to my uncle,
asked if he was all right, he looked at me
with his one good eye, and I knew he saw
just another Indian, no better than the slaves
or his other livestock fenced inside their pens.

Henrietta (Cherokee Freedwoman—b. 1852)

When I was ten, living on the plantation of Colonel Adair,
Northern soldiers rode up one day, promised us slaves
they were there to set us free, let us live just like the white
folks with our own houses and farms. They rounded up
every horse and cow they could corral and started driving
them, and us, to Kansas. There were only a hundred
slaves when we left Tahlequah, but four or five times
that when we reached the Kansas line. The Negro men
joined the Union Army, and the women were put to work
in the fields. Freedom felt a lot like the life we had left.
We thought the livestock we drove from the Territory
would be split among us to give us a start, but we never
saw the herds again. The soldiers imprisoned my master,
William Penn Adair, until his trial at Fort Leavenworth.
But after he spoke in his own defense, they set him free,
and he went home to join Stand Watie's Confederates
until the war ended. My family returned to Fourteen
Mile Creek in '66, back to the people who once owned
us, but who now counted us as a part of their own.

Sally (Anglo—b. 1869)

Father would sit still as a stone
at the well, waiting for the bees
to sip from the trough nearby,
storing water in their crops
before ferrying it home to the hive.
Once they took flight, a line
of buzz back to a hollow tree
or rock crevice, he would follow
through white clover, goldenrod,
milkweed. He only stole from them
in June or early July, giving time
to make more sweetness before frost.

He would build a small, brushy fire
near the entrance, then once the bees
were stunned, he used his knife
to break the comb, mining for gold,
letting it ooze inside a metal pan
like the forty-niners used.
In years since, I have learned
that bees only live about a month
in the wild, only make a thimbleful
of honey in a lifetime. Imagine that—
a whole life inside a thimble.

Hattie (Cherokee—b. 1840)

We always buried our dead in the ground,
not like other tribes I have heard about
who built platforms of wood, left the bodies
to bake in sun or freeze in snow, or those
who took their dying to the hills, knowing
their remains would be pecked and gnawed.
No, we buried our dead in the earth
until we arrived in the Territory, rife with wild
animals—coyotes, sending up their cries to the night
skies, and wolves, pacing and pawing at dust.
So we took up the boards of our cabin floor,
dug a hole to keep the dead safe. We placed
little belongings inside the grave—a hairbrush,
a bracelet, a lucky buckeye—so we would not see
these precious things lying about and be filled
with sadness. As a girl, I remember my grandmother
being laid beneath the slats, the *tap, tap* of hammer
nailing them back in place. For days, when I walked
through the room, I thought I heard her knocking,
scratching at the wood underneath my feet, begging me
to pull up the boards, welcome her back to the living.

Violet (Anglo—b. 1868)

An Indian man, crippled with time, lived beside us.
We children would draw near him, would draw
cool water from the well, hold the dripping gourd
for him. When he died, his people dug a grave
larger than any we had ever seen. The mourners
filed 'round the hole and threw beans, blankets,
trinkets inside, along with the old man's trousers,
shirts, a pair of doe-hide shoes. Finally, one of the band
led a Paint horse to the opening—his head
near the feet of the dead—his spotted skin quivering
as if he knew. A young Indian man drew a pistol,
raised it. With one blast, the horse fell at the edge
of the pit. A rope was looped around the pony's neck,
and the men pushed and pulled the beast down
on top of the man's body. Each member took turns
dipping a small white cloth into the pinto's blood,
then folded it carefully, placed it in their pockets
or inside their bodices. That Paint never made a sound,
but in my dreams, I saw the scene over and over,
heard a piercing scream that was always my own.

Ola (Chickasaw—b. No birth date)

My mother's mother was Cherokee, and she lived
with us in the Caddo Hills. At night, she would put
us children to bed, in winter, warming a linsey wool
quilt before the fire, smoothing it over us like soil
covering the seeds in her garden. She spent her spring
and summer days hoeing around tender corn and squash
plants, discouraging deer by spreading our dogs' fur
around her furrows. Even when working outside,
she wore hoops inside her skirts, perhaps a remnant
of the Southern life she once lived. But when it stormed,
she removed the rings, fearing that the steel would draw
lightning, licking against her skirts with flaming tongues.
My sister and I borrowed little knives from our brothers,
cut briar branches, just the right length, then spent
a day carving away the sharp barbs. Finally, we bent,
shaped them to fit inside the casing. When we were done,
Grandmother stood outside in her briar skirts, looked
up at the darkening sky, defied the fire to find her.

Nettie (Cherokee—b. 1851)

They were called Pins because they tucked
cross pins under the collars of their coats
or fastened them to the chests of their calico
shirts, worn with turbans—dress most men
in our Nation had traded for suits and hats.
Born from a secret society, this group
was made up of Cherokee Unionists,
followers of the Red Path—blood revenge—
which they sought to heap upon us
Cherokee Confederates. When I
was no more than twelve, they stopped
at the gate of Abe Woodall, our neighbor,
called him to the door, and shot him
without ever dismounting. That same day—
before we heard they were going to burn
down our house;
before my mother carried the husk
of my father, wasting away for weeks,
to a nearby cave;
before I stumbled behind her,
his featherbed and pillows in tow;
before we saw the night sky glow
with embers—
the Pins rode into our yard, grabbed Uncle Thomas
from the porch, and while my sisters and I
watched from the windows, they slit open
his chest with a hunting knife, took out
his heart, still beating, and for a few seconds
I saw the Devil holding the Blood Moon
in his mighty hands.

Edna (Anglo—No birth date)

Just like long ago when kings had their food
tested before they let it pass their lips,
we had Jim, a bird dog with brown freckles, good
at pin-pointing poison. One or two sniffs,
and he would let us know whether eating
what I had fixed was advisable. Coons,
quail, rabbits, prairie chickens—everything
I dressed and cooked—I offered to Jim. Soon
as I put before him a heaping plate,
he would gobble it down, but once I caught
a possum in my hen coop. Varmint ate
a heap of eggs, but I finally shot
him, soaked him with salt, roasted until brown.
Jim whiffed, yelped, buried his nose in the ground.

Alberta (Anglo—b. 1862)

I settled a farm in Geary with Mr. Emmet
Langtree, my first husband, until Mr. Emmet
grew homesick for Kansas, and I grew
sick of Mr. Emmet. I started cooking
for the Choctaw Railroad, forty-five
or fifty men per meal, and I was there
when the first train chugged into town,
black smoke like a hornet swarm.
We women placed tatted hankies
over our noses but lost our primness,
waving welcome to the handsome engineer,
signaling a surrender of propriety.

Looking back, my fondest memory?
The Cherokee Strip—great salt plains,
spread out like a white enamel table top,
sparking in the sunlight, people scooping
shovels full, heaping crystals into wagons.
Just once, I saw a herd of Texas longhorns
stampede through the Strip, their hooves
churning, turning ground into swirling flakes,
a blizzard that rose from the summer earth
in a flurry of saline clouds before drifting
down again, softly, like tattered lace.

Inola (Cherokee—b. 1887)

I married my Henry when I was seventeen.
That next April, we were breaking ground
for our garden when the sycamore leaves
fluttered a warning, flipped over,
surrendered to the angry skies
just as the birds hushed their song.
Henry grabbed my hand, and we ran
to the creek slope, lay flat on rocks
as a cyclone swept through Craig County.
It rowed right up the Grand River
at noon, picking the country as clean
as a chicken bone. On the north bank
stood the Thompson mansion, made
by slaves who molded and burned
the bricks on site. The twister pointed
its finger, and when the sky cleared,
windows were shattered, walls fallen
to rubble. A week later, we bought the bricks
cheap, and Henry tore them apart
with an old file blade, while I cut loose
the mortar and stacked till my hands
were bleeding and raw. We filled the wagon,
over and over, hauled them to our land,
where they rose again like Lazarus.
On the morning we moved into our home,
my mother first brought in a sack of meal,
for food a plenty, and then a Bible,
so we would have a Christian home,
but I whispered to the air *wado,* thank you,
just in case Wind still spoke the old tongue.

Florence (Anglo—b. 1881)

When we first moved to the Territory,
I was charmed by the wild creatures—
squirrels chasing and chattering
through the trees, while possums
and coons came right up to the cabin
door, begging for scraps. Even the snakes,
since we had no rattlers, did not bother
me as they sunned themselves in the road.
And the wolves moved like smoke
through the sycamores—there one moment,
then gone—gray vapor. But birds began to weigh
on me—a strange thing to say since they
sail on air with their hollow bones.
Woodpeckers drove us to distraction
as their scarlet heads see-sawed up and down,
pounding their beaks into the logs of our home.
And the crows, with their shiny eyes,
sat and waited for the corn plants to break
through the ground before swooping down,
plucking them all by the root. But worst
for me were the doves, who in the spring,
sat on the rooftop, made a sound so lonesome,
I longed to go home to my mother, to leave
behind this land I did not yet understand.

Cora (Choctaw Freedwoman—b. 1857)

This land is home, has been since
long before the Choctaws adopted
us, called us their own. I live alone
in this old shack. Back when
I first moved here, a log house stood
on this spot, but it decided to return
to the dirt like we all will someday.
I got me this second-hand house,
more than forty years ago now,
and an old Negro named Matt Freeman
made boards for the roof when we rebuilt it.
He lives near Sawyer now, must be ninety
or more. When the Choctaws claimed us,
they gave us each forty acres. Growing
up, I never owned more than a homespun dress,
straw hat, and a cowrie shell necklace
my mama brought from Virginia
when she was sold to a Tennessee planter.
So I rode to Sulphur Springs all by myself
to stake my claim in court, make this place mine.
And when I die, I will still be here
in my house on my land—*mine,*
a word that sings in my mouth
like some sweet old Baptist hymn.

Augusta (Anglo—b. 1857)

I sang a song to myself:

Oh, I am going to starvation land,
Oh, I am going to starvation land,
But if I ford the roiling Red River,
I will never cross back again.

We sold our cotton, and we sold
our corn, still tasseling in our fields.
Sold our land for half its worth
and chartered a railroad car
to haul five hundred jars of fruit
and preserves, lard, meat, two mules,
one mare.

I caught the train to Vernon, Texas,
my seven small ones in tow,
then took a wagon to the Territory,
jostling into the unknown.
When we finally made it to the banks
of the wide water, my heart was filled
with quicksand.

Oh, I am going to starvation land,
Oh, I am going to starvation land,
But if I ford the roiling Red River,
I can never cross back again.

Jennie (Choctaw/Chickasaw—b. 1883)

My grandmother grew up in the Arbuckle Mountains,
granite and limestone cliffs cradling
redbuds and ribbon falls during spring run-off.
Her parents homesteaded there, a place
too rocky for grain but perfect for grazing
cattle, for gazing out on some of the prettiest
land God ever made.

After sixty years, she still cried remembering
one day when she and Nettie, her best friend,
rode toward a neighbor's house, five miles
away, a neighbor who was the envy
of the valley because she owned a sewing
machine. The girls stretched their fabric
across the saddles, just behind the horn,
to keep the cloth from wrinkling.

Not far from home, they spotted a herd
of horses, driven by a man they thought
must be a slave, and Nettie called out
to Grandmother that they should race him.
But as they drew near, the man let out
a wildcat's call—Comanche—a name
that meant "enemy."

A band of Indians bore down on them
from the hills. The girls jerked their reins
round, tried to ride back to the cabins,
but the Paint horses were faster.
My grandmother jumped from her saddle—
material fluttering to the dust—
and let her horse run on as she hid

in the tall prairie bushes—bluestem,
turkey foot, switchgrass. As the Comanche
raced by, one hung from his mount
and snatched the cloth, while she held
her breath, curled into herself, hoping
that if she closed her own eyes,
he would not see her.

She heard the shot, then the herd racing away—
now with two more horses. She could not say
how long she lay there before rising,
running back home, and finding Nettie,
shot in the back, blood spilling outside
her front door, the girl still clutching
to her chest the cloth for her burial dress.

Rose (Anglo—b. 1870)

This part of Atoka County was rough and rocky,
with high bluffs and caves covered in pine
and oak timber. Some places, a person
had to travel afoot or on horseback,
so outlaws and robbers rested here
unmolested by the law. Cole Younger—
once pardoned or paroled—toured
the states, making speeches to young
people in churches. When he spoke
to us in Atoka, he told about a nearby cave
where he and the James boys lived
for six months. Located in the side
of a mountain, the cave had a stream
that ran near its mouth, flowing east
into Potapo Creek. A large boulder
had fallen down, blocking the view
of the entrance. Late evenings and early
mornings, bobcats and wolves would come
from their dens, play in the prairie
glade. Nearby was Kennedy Hollow,
where Belle Starr, once Younger's
lover and mother of his daughter,
hung out with her crew. And on the east
of McGee Creek, the Mathews and Brown
gangs hid out. In later years, a man
I know named Arthur Goad told the story
of taking shelter from the rain
inside one of the caves. When he noticed
loose clay on the floor beneath a stone,

he dug it out and found inside a leather
pouch stuffed with seven hundred dollars,
the most money Arthur had ever seen.
He remembered Cole Younger's speech
about crime not paying, and Art always smiled
when he told the tale.

Nannie (Cherokee—b. 1877)

When I opened the door, there he was—
sitting astride a Paint horse, its nose
thrust over the threshold. The man was huge,
Osage, his ears split and hung with keys,
his head as painted as his pinto. He spoke
no English but held up an American dime,
pointed to a pile of sweet potatoes stacked
by the door. My baby clutched to my chest,
I pushed past him and ran to the field
where John, my husband, was clearing brush.
Blade in hand, he led me back to the cabin.
The Osage waited. We sold him a gunny
sack full, just as several wagons, loaded
with Osage women and children, jostled by.
The man whirled his horse and followed
but soon circled back, pounding his sack
of potatoes. I thought him angry or crazed,
but a young boy jumped down from a wagon
and in bits of English explained they wanted
more sweet potatoes to feed their people,
eyes speaking the language of starvation.
Women opened bundles they carried,
eager to trade. Inside were stacks of government
calico—yards and yards of tiny meadow
flowers—and I hurried to the dugout
where our stores were kept, my fingers
trembling at the thought of stitches and seams,
the dresses I would sew from the fabric
of their misery.

Lizzie (Anglo—b. 1867)

Before we bought lumber in Lawton
and built our home on Blue Beaver Creek,
we lived in two tents, one for kitchen
and dining, the other for sleeping and living.
Afraid to stay alone, I was happy when neighbors
stopped by. And they were eager to exchange time
for apples, plucked fresh from our orchard,
or butter, churned each morning, too abundant
for a couple without children. One day,
two Indian women came to call, asking
with gestures to see how I cooked, their hands
stirring imaginary pots. I gave each a fresh
biscuit, spread with wild blackberry jam,
watched as they smiled, nodded. Motioning
for them to sit, I opened my camelback
trunk, hauled all the way from Kentucky,
and pulled out my family photograph
album, covered with velvet, and the women
stroked the cover gently, like a living thing.
When I opened the book, they both started,
seeing in front of them a picture of me,
taken on my wedding day. They pointed
back and forth from my face, to the picture,
awed by the miracle, some act of God,
that could have made my face appear
in two places. I did not have the words
to explain how a camera could capture
a person's image, and I am sure the women
left, wondering what other magic
this white witch could conjure.

Winema (Modoc—b. 1872)

We were driven from Oregon in 1875.
I was only three, so I have no memory
of the months aboard the wagon,
the mountains and rivers we crossed
to reach our prairie prison. My mother
and father died soon after our arrival,
so I do not remember them either, except
for some passing scent that sometimes
makes the word *mother* still form on my lips
although I am an old woman now. My parents
are buried inside the Modoc cemetery,
where some plots are marked with monuments,
peonies and rosebushes crowning the heads
of the dead. But the old graves on top
of a silent knoll contain remains of those
who sickened and died when we reached
this place, those who passed from heartache
and grief, more deadly than fever, famine.
There are two rows, marked only by native
rock, sandstone slabs, pried from the earth
to stand upright, heavenward. Today, no one knows
one grave from another, all equal in death,
anonymous as the dust they have become.

Vera (Anglo—b. 1872)

My brother John lived in Greer County, eight miles
from Granite, west of the rugged Gyp Hills. I loved
visiting his old home, dug out from the ground
and covered with dirt. Out front was a brush arbor,
trellis roofed with dry foliage, where we would sit
in the evening, the coolest place on the prairie.
One night, as we headed to bed, John picked up
his sons, no older than three or four, draped them across
his shoulders, ducked as he went through the door.
As soon as he laid the boys on their bed,
he heard the singing of a rattlesnake's song.

> He told his wife to get his gun.
> He told me to hold the lamp.
> He told the boys not to move.

John raised the gun in the dim light of the dugout,
inhaled, squeezed the trigger. For a long moment,
before the blast echoed off the sod walls,
before our ears rang to deafness,
before the single shot took the head right off
the snake as it lay coiled between the boys,
we were all still as a posed photograph,
not knowing what story we would be telling
in years to come, what kind of ending it would have.

Josie (Cherokee—b. 1887)

One time, my father and Thomas Buffington, six-foot-
tall Cherokee chief with long black hair, who lived
on a farm near ours in Vinita, took a load of wheat
to Southwest City across the border in Missouri.
Coming home with sacks of bran and two gallons
of illegal liquor, they were stopped by U.S.
Marshalls, but not before Buffington poured
the libation upon the sacks. One officer, eyeing
the rifle riding between the two men, stuck
a hand under the cover, gave them a nod,
and rode off. When my father and his friend
reached home, they took two wide planks,
stuck them in the cracks of a log cabin,
and squeezed out enough whiskey for their
Christmas toast. The hogs that ate the bran
were also said to stumble a bit, and one,
they swore, danced a jig.

Iva (Anglo—b. 1855)

My husband went away before daylight on his way
to Quanah, while I, confined to our dugout
with a nine-month-old baby, waited his return,
counting the hours—two days, one night.
When the sun set on the prairie, a spark of orange
and gold before fading to black, I lit a lamp,
tucked the babe into his cradle, and bent over
my mending in the dim light. My eyes, shuttered
in slumber, flew open, and my sewing slipped
from my lap when I heard the scratching,
scratching, scratching. Sam, my little terrier,
barked once then tucked his tail and hid beneath
the bed. *Scratch. Scratch. Scratch.* My husband
had taken the one gun we owned. The only
weapon I held was prayer. And still the scratching,
scratching, scratching went on all night, while I
waited for daylight. When the first gleam broke,
I peeked out through the hole now open
in the roof. A panther, twenty feet long
from tip to tip, gave one last scratch, met
my eyes, found me unworthy, and was gone.

Lottie (Choctaw Freedwoman—b. 1859)

I am one-fourth Choctaw and the rest colored,
but I have lived my life among the Creek Indians.

Out of all the men who resided in Creek Nation—
outlaws, killers, robbers—the most dangerous,
most feared, was a full-blood by the name
of Wesley Barnett. Schooled at Haskell Institute,
but taught to kill by his step-father, for two weeks
Wesley sulked like a rattlesnake outside his mother's house,
waiting with his rifle, seeking revenge for her death, gunned down
when she refused to take her husband back. When Wesley's
step-father finally stepped outside, Barnett emptied
his rifle into the man, shooting again and again,
even after he was dead. But Barnett was never
taken to jail since justice was served.

Twelve years passed, Wesley wandering from place
to place. He married an Indian woman and settled
close to Eufaula, where one day a stomp dance
was being held. He rode off, leaving his bride
behind, but later his brother arrived with Wesley's
wife in a wagon, and so enraged him that he shot
his own blood in the back as he went to the spring
to drink. Barnett knew he could not beat the law,
so he rode to Okmulgee, bought two coffins—
one for his brother and one for himself.

But two years later, he was still free,
shooting at the wing of the eagle that eternally
perched on the top of the Creek Council House,
running with train robbers. The law tried to surprise them while
they were counting their take one day,

45

but Wesley's horse was trained to stamp
its front feet at the least noise, and the two
were speeding away before the gang was aware
of danger. Pursued by the lawmen, Barnett
turned on his horse, leveled his Winchester,
and picked them off like prairie chickens.

He headed for Arkansas before returning
to his wife, who feared for her own life.
One night, while Wesley was out, a friend
of his wife waited behind a barrel
inside their cabin, and when Wesley
entered after midnight, the man blasted
Barnett in the face with a shotgun.
He ran to his horse, mounted, then fell
to the ground. We all breathed a sigh
of relief. It is a lot easier to love the legend.

Sadie (Anglo—b. 1889)

The year Oklahoma claimed statehood,
my husband and his brother, Charles,
started building our first home.
They hacked away with shovels
and pick axes, creating a cloud
of red dust that rose and hung
in the air, the only clouds we saw
for months. The men carved
a dugout into the side of a bank,
covered the crude cave with bark,
stripped from catalpa trees, cottonwoods.
But when we moved in, placed
my mama's old rocker on the earthen
floor, along with the table and caned
chairs we had hauled from Kentucky,
the dirt fell and sifted through cracks
in the wooden slats. I mixed flour
and water to a paste, plastered the walls
and ceiling with pages from the *Cimarron
News*. Behind the paper sheets,
I could hear the bugs and spiders
scurrying around the stories. Driven
to distraction, I stabbed scissors
through the print, slicing a centipede,
impaling a tarantula. Always listening,
listening for the unmistakable rattle.

Inez (Choctaw—b. No birth date)

My grandmother would come to visit us in summer
and stay until the persimmons ripened into amber moons.
She sat in the corner like a spider and spun
her stories of coming to the Territory when she was eight,
forced to walk on the Trail. Everybody who was able
had to walk, and if babies collapsed from fatigue,
or their parents were too ill to carry them,
drivers of the ox wagons would swing the little ones,
cracking their heads against tree trunks, leaving them
by the roadside, unburied like feral dogs.
Joel, her brother, was only four, and his chubby
little legs could not keep up the pace.
So she carried him, his fingers clinging
to her neck, his knees clenched around
her waist. Her muscles burned with his weight,
the strain of mile after mile. And when she
could no longer hold him, he climbed onto her back,
his arms encircling her neck, his breath
warm and sweet, breaths that she learned
to count with each step—just one more, just one more.

Pearl (Anglo—b. 1870)

I named my pony Stockings
because of his four white feet—
like a little girl's lacy anklets—
and those sturdy feet took me,
side saddle, from Texas
to the Red River. In those days,
all ladies rode side saddle. Crossing
on Bounds Ferry, we lodged
against a sandbar halfway across.
I whispered sweet words to Stockings,
stroked his mane, and mounted.

We forged our own current
through the river, scrambled
up the bank of the Territory,
waiting for the wagons
to follow—buckboard boats
with full sails. It would be the last
we would see of water for days
to come, until I spied a spring
some distance from the road,
too much green not to be fed
from below. I told the others
to go on. Once my jug was filled,
I led my pony back through the brush
to meet the wagons, but even the dust
that followed them like a haint was gone.

Blocking the path, two Indians on foot—
the first I had ever seen—
their skin as tanned as my saddle,
hair the color of crows.

There was no place to go. Forgetting
manners, I mounted like a man,
lashed Stockings with my quirt,
and galloped through them, my riding skirt
flapping like the wings of a hunted quail,
flushed to flight.

Birdie (Cherokee—b. 1877)

We feared the cows had found their way
through the broken fence to Panther Hollow,
a place filled with oaks—green acorns
just waiting with their poison. My husband,
laid up with pneumonia, was too weak
to leave the cabin, so I took my daughter Nora
with me, and we set out to bring them home.
Carrying sticks, we called to them by name—
Bess, Gert, Belle. But dark fell early
in the hollers, and before we knew it,
we were lost. I told Nora not to be afraid,
but a knot formed around my heart
as shadows deepened. Just then,
we thought we heard my husband calling
for us, and we followed his voice,
tripping over roots, tangling with briars.
But when we broke through the undergrowth,
before us was a set of amber eyes, sleek
black body, and a voice luring us closer.
Breathless, we froze in tracks until
the night was blasted open by both barrels
of a shotgun. The cat became liquid,
ink fading into the trees. We followed
the loud report home, where the cows
waited for us near the barn, lowing,
as if mourning what could have been.

Sarah (Anglo—b. 1874)

Feathers must be sunned, hanging—
like fletchings of spent arrows—
for six months or more, then trapped
inside muslin sacks to cure. Green
feathers inside a thick ticking
will sicken you with their smell
of carnage. For nine years, I chased
my geese through the woods,
tripping over roots of bur oak,
sycamore, then sat on the porch
picking ticks and bramble thorns.
In the end, I came away with feather
beds for my eight living sons,
twenty-two pillows, and a softness
in my heart for the sacrificed.

Mary (Euchee—b. Between 1846-1851)

I was born near Polecat Creek,
but I do not know the year.
My parents died when I was small,
so there was no one to tell me,
Today is the day you first joined
the Long Tiger Band, our family.

I did learn the ways of my people.
Some might call them superstitions,
but there is much we do not understand.
Always take care at night. Never
let baby clothes hang outside
on the line after sunset, or the babe
may become bewitched. Do not
throw out dish water in the dark,
or your grandmother will rise
from her grave to take you.
When someone dies, do not
travel at night to reach him,
for the spirits upon the earth
will sicken you, take you, too.

But there are other warnings
for daytime. Never throw your hair
outside on the ground for the birds
to gather and weave into a nest,
or you will suffer great headaches.
Do not burn the hair off any person,
or God will punish you, making you
hunt for the torched hair before gaining
forgiveness of your sin. When wading,

watch out for Tie-Snakes, larger
and stronger than water moccasins,
that will pull you under, hold you forever.
Some will call these superstitions.
To me—my heart, my bones, my blood.

Dora (Anglo—b. 1855)

I always called my husband Mr. Rexing
because I first knew him as a widower
neighbor whose wife had died birthing
their first child—three years before
he courted me—and by the time he asked
for my hand, I could not bring myself
to call him Frank. When we left Illinois
for the Territory, Mr. R. drove a covered
wagon, filled with farm implements, feed,
two chairs, and a stove. I drove
a covered spring wagon with the children,
chickens, turkeys, and a pen with two pigs.
To the bows, I fastened two cages with a pair
of yellow canary birds. Every day,
Louis, our eldest, would whistle the same
tune, urging the birds to sing, but they sat,
silent. We arrived on the fifth of September,
and one month to the day, we buried Louis,
only eleven years old. I had no time to mourn
his loss when my husband and the other three
young ones were wracked with raging
typhoid fever. For eight weeks, I pressed
cool cloths to brows, rubbed aching legs,
wiped away sickness, my days and nights
a blur of hauling water, boiling water,
knowing that bad water was what brought
us this misery. Each evening I prayed
to the God I hoped had followed us here,
and one morning I woke to my canaries,
singing the tune Louis had whistled
all the way to this wretched wasteland.

Mahala (Cherokee—b. 1877)

You should never eat Devil's Shoestring,
but the root, in your pocket, does bring you luck,
a charm to ward off evil. When I was young,
Cherokees used it, borrowing the Creek ways
of fishing in a group. Each man toted a mallet,
a hickory post four or five feet tall with one end
carved to a point, and a bundle of the roots, gray
and twisted like fingers of the dead. The men
would find a deep hole in a creek, then drive
their posts, forming a circle like a stomp dance.
They put the Devil's Shoestring on top
of the posts and began to beat the root
in rhythm, making a sound like croaking
of spring frogs. They drummed until juice
ran out and washed into the water.
Fish would float to the surface, scales
catching the sun, and fishermen, armed
with bows and arrows, would be waiting.
If a fish decided to dive for its life,
a man would go under, too, rising
from the depths, dripping, holding
silver in his hands. We women watched
from the bank, waiting with a kettle
of hot lard for frying, but I wanted
to be one of them, one of the fishermen,
making a music so sweet that even
a fish with no ears was lured to sacrifice.

Maggie (Anglo—b. 1868)

More than Indians, we feared prairie fires.
The grasses grew six feet tall, and winter
turned them dry, brittle as old bird bones.
The wind would let loose a wild whoosh
of fury, and the flames would run and jump,
skipping streams, trapping anyone
or anything not fast enough to flee.
One Christmas morning, a boy, too young
to understand his actions, struck a match,
dropped it into a brown tuft. A tornado
of flames formed, sending thunderheads
of smoke across the sky. Men from miles
away saw the red message written
above the plains and came in wagons
loaded with barrels of water and burlap
bags, ready to be soaked. They slapped
the sparks, tried to smother this living,
breathing witch fire that grew with each
gust, crackling like laughter. Tears
streaming down soiled faces and lungs
full of fear, the men toiled on. At last,
the flames died to charred earth
and gray wisps. We women brought
out Christmas dinners intended for our own,
and we bowed our heads, thanking God—
not for what we had been given,
but for what had not been taken away.

Nell (Delaware—b. No birth date)

Albert Whiteturkey, my brother, was married
to Julia Johnson for nigh on eight years
before she left him to marry a Cherokee
named Gilstrap, an outlaw shot down
in a general store shortly after. But she
must have liked men of adventure
because she next married Ernest Lewis,
another bandit, killed on Statehood Day
in Bartlesville. A few years later,
Julia wed Emmet Dalton, called "Em,"
the youngest of the gang, who started out
working as a deputy and a cowboy
at Bar X Bar Ranch in the Pawnee Agency,
but spent close to fifteen years in prison
for his part in the Coffeyville, Kansas,
robbery of the First National Bank,
where he left with a grain sack stuffed
with over twenty thousand dollars,
but ended up with twenty-three lead slugs
throughout his body and the fresh corpses
of two brothers and two friends, posed
for pictures in the streets. Of course,
all of that mess was before Julia married Em,
who wrote books about his life of crime,
moved to Hollywood, became a star
for being one of the last of the Wild West
desperadoes. And I hate to admit, I was a little
bit jealous of Julia for ending up with Em,
a dangerous man, handsome enough
to make a Christian woman blush.

Helen (Anglo—b. 1855)

My friends from Coldwater, the place in Ohio
where we lived before we made the move
to the Territory, would come to visit in the early
days, before friendships faded like a dress
worn and washed too many times. Once, I took
my visitors to Darlington, where the Indians
camped. But when the tribe crowded around us,
clapping on our backs, all speaking in a tongue
still strange even to me, my friends froze
in fear, not knowing if they welcomed us
or planned to carry our scalps on sticks.
I smiled, and they gestured for us to follow
their group to the North Canadian, the summer
heat baking our backs as we sat on the bank.
The Indians were teaching their young
to swim in the river, still swollen from spring
rains. They picked up their babies, no older
than two, threw them into the water. The little
fellows would bob to the surface and paddle
back to the bank, their hair as slick as otter
pelts. Sometimes the elders would throw twigs,
telling the children to bring them back.
Over and over, this terrifying game played
out, until the children were swimming
like carp. But my white friends covered
their mouths to keep their screams
of *barbarians* buried inside their throats.

Ruby (Chickasaw—b. 1837)

It was hard to be a woman in those early days.
Our lives were only worth the price a man
gave us. If a husband decided his wife
was a weight on his neck, a burdensome
stone, there was always somebody willing
to lighten his load for a few coins. And more
than likely, the law turned a blind eye.
My husband's half-sister, Martha Willis,
was taking some quilt pieces to her mother
one day. Mr. Willis sent a man and a boy,
whom his wife did not know, to accompany her,
with word that he would follow. A week later,
Martha's broken body was found lodged
on a rock in Little River. All around her
lay strewn quilt blocks—washed upon the shore—
stitched in the Double Wedding Ring pattern.

Ruth (Anglo—b. No birth date)

Being the baby of the family, I was my father's
constant companion from the time I was born.
When I was four, the Cherokee Strip was thrown
open for us whites who moved onto the land
like grasshoppers on corn. When my father
decided to make the "run," he insisted
that I go, too, leaving my mother to wring
her hands in her apron as she stood
in the doorway, watching as we started off
for Kiowa, Kansas, to spend the night.

Next morning, all of the wagons brimmed
the border, and at high noon, the firing
of guns signaled the start of the land run.
Father drove a team hitched to a spring
wagon, while I stood at the front, holding
the dashboard, the skirts of my dark blue
calico dress whipping around my legs,
my bonnet bouncing against my back,
its knots holding tight.

The world around me was dust and noise—
shouting to mounts, whips on horse flesh,
cursing and grinding of wood as the wagons
crowded against each other. When my father
spotted a place he liked, a spot that looked
like all the others to me, he leapt from the rig
while I handed him the stakes and hammer.

Then I held the horses' reins while he drove
his claim home, and we never thought of those
others, the ones who had lived on this land
for so many years that their titles
were written in the soil itself, signed
with generations of blood.

Beulah (Cherokee/Chickasaw—b. 1837)

Just because we were removed from the South
does not mean the South was removed from us.
During the War Between the States, I helped
my mother hide our food and our bedding,
from bands of Northern soldiers, locusts in blue,
who would take everything they could carry.
But we held a soft spot for the Southerners
who spoke like sorghum was dripping from their lips.
We parched meal and wheat to make coffee,
parched sweet potato hulls. The soldiers, parched
and starving, lined up single file, taking a piece
of meat, a slab of bread, nodding and thanking
us, never cursing when all was gone before
they were fed. But the Union men looked down
their Northern noses at us, Indian women, less than
human in their eyes. They raided our cellar,
taking away every last turnip we had hidden,
never stopping to think what might become of us,
never knowing about the other stashes that kept
us and the boys in grey alive, fighting until
even Stand Watie, last general to surrender,
woke to the truth that our hopes were as barren
as our trampled cornfields, our leafless gardens.

Tillie (Cherokee—b. 1887)

Vinita was a rough and tough place
in the early days. We hardly dared
to keep a light burning in our house,
or some outlaw would ride by and use it
for target practice. As soon as dark fell,
we pulled our blinds so as not to invite
prying eyes. Rowdies would raid
our farm lot, kill a fat hog, cut out a ham,
and leave the rest to flies. One day
as I was out riding, searching for cattle
that had gone astray, I rode past a group
of men butchering our beef, their shirts
covered in sweat and blood. One glance,
and then I turned my head, nudged my horse
to a trot. It did not pay to see too much,
to talk too much, to know too much.

Esther (Anglo—b. 1883)

In the summertime, blackberry season,
our mother would rub our legs and arms
with sulfur-dosed lard, dress us in long
sleeves—even though the heat plastered
our shirts to our backs—trying to fend off
ticks and chiggers. But what we feared
most were the wild hogs, snuffling
and roaring, their teeth popping
as they ate their way through brambles,
traveling in packs, stampeding through
the forest. Two neighbor women
took turns walking us the three miles
to Thomasville to sell our berries,
fifteen cents a gallon. One told a story
of how her cousin, when a child,
headed to his aunt's house but never
arrived. When the family finally found
him, the hogs had left only his hands,
his feet, and his bones, picked so clean
they could have been carved into flutes.

Awinita (Cherokee—b. 1878)

My mother told me stories—
    how the white neighbors
    barged through their cabin door
    while her pa was plowing
    the field. How they staked
    their claim to the butter churn,
    a looking glass inside plaster frame,
    a rocker made of willow, soaked
    and bent by her grandfather's hands.
    They swore they would return, the only
    promise the whites ever kept—greedy
    vultures swooping in after soldiers
    bearing ropes, rifles, bayonets.

My mother told me stories—
    how they were driven to stockades,
    taking only what they could carry—
    dented cooking pot, extra calico
    dress, star quilt stitched from family
    scraps. How they clung to each other
    in the dirt, comforting the children,
    babies crying at dry breasts,
    mothers given nothing more
    than a sack of weevil-ridden flour
    that they did not know how to cook.
    How fever swept through the camp
    like a prairie wildfire in drought.

My mother told me stories—
  how Levi Kemp led the colony
  like a herd of broken cattle,
  prodded when their pace slowed,
  fed two cups of hot water, corn bread,
  one turnip a day. They ate bark
  from the slippery elm when hunger
  became a howling wolf. How for two
  months of misery they marched—cold
  marrowing their bones. Bones of the dead
  were left beneath stones when the ground
  was too frozen to dig. No time to mourn
  the lost when living was the greater sorrow.

My mother told me stories—
  how the elders prayed for a sign
  to sustain their people as hope
  sprouted talons and wings,
  flew away like a red-tailed hawk.
  How all the way to Fort Washita
  the people could hear a great roaring
  deep within the ground, as if earth
  bore witness, bemoaned her people's pain.
  How all along the trail, sandstone rocks
  shaped like Georgia roses appeared
  upon the ground wherever a tear
  tumbled down to touch the soil.

About the Author

Linda Neal Reising, a native of Oklahoma and a member of the Western Cherokee Nation, has been published in numerous journals, including *The Southern Indiana Review, The Comstock Review,* and *Nimrod.* Reising's work has also appeared in a number of anthologies, including *Fruitflesh: Seeds of Inspiration for Women Who Write* (Harper/Collins) and *And Know This Place: Poetry of Indiana* (Indiana Historical Society Press). She was named the winner of the 2012 Writer's Digest Poetry Competition. Her chapbook, *Re-Writing Family History* (Finishing Line Press), was a finalist for the 2015 Oklahoma Book Award, as well as winner of the 2015 Oklahoma Writers' Federation Poetry Book Prize. In 2018, her work was nominated for a Pushcart Prize by the editors of *So It Goes: The Literary Journal of the Kurt Vonnegut Museum & Library. The Keeping,* her first full-length book of poetry, was published by Finishing Line Press in 2020.

Made in the USA
Monee, IL
24 November 2021

82918973R00039